GW00367937

ALWAYS LOOK

ON THE

BRIGHT SIDE

summersdale

ALWAYS LOOK ON THE BRIGHT SIDE

First published as *Always Look on the Bright Side of Life* in 2014

Research by Sarah Viner

An Hachette UK Company
www.hachette.co.uk

Summersdale Publishers Ltd
Part of Octopus Publishing Group Limited
Carmelite House
50 Victoria Embankment
LONDON
EC4Y 0DZ
UK

www.summersdale.com

Printed and bound in the Czech Republic

ISBN: 978-1-78685-023-2

Substantial discounts on bulk quantities of Summersdale books are available to corporations, professional associations and other organisations. For details contact general enquiries: telephone: +44 (0) 1243 771107 or email: enquiries@summersdale.com.

TO. . . . .

FROM. . . . .

KEEP SMILING,
BECAUSE LIFE IS A
BEAUTIFUL THING AND
THERE'S SO MUCH
TO SMILE ABOUT.

MARILYN MONROE

It is always the simple that produces the marvellous.

AMELIA BARR

MUDDY WATER,
LET STAND,
BECOMES CLEAR.

LAO TZU

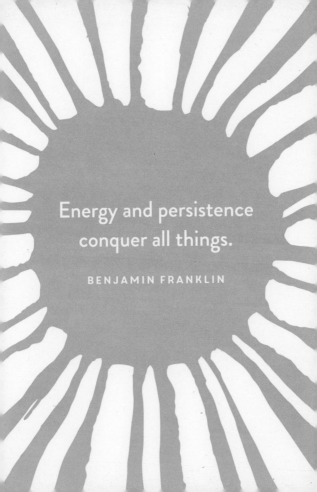

Energy and persistence
conquer all things.

BENJAMIN FRANKLIN

The best thing to
hold on to in life
is each other.

AUDREY HEPBURN

THE MORE WE DO,
THE MORE WE CAN DO.

WILLIAM HAZLITT

**LOOK ON EVERY
EXIT AS BEING
AN ENTRANCE
SOMEWHERE ELSE.**

TOM STOPPARD

A smile is a curve that
sets everything straight.

PHYLLIS DILLER

Every day brings a chance for you to draw in a breath, kick off your shoes... and dance.

OPRAH WINFREY

THE WAY I SEE IT,
IF YOU WANT THE
RAINBOW, YOU
GOTTA PUT UP
WITH THE RAIN.

DOLLY PARTON

This life is not for complaint,
but for satisfaction.

HENRY DAVID THOREAU

You can't expect to hit the jackpot if you don't put a few nickels in the machine.

FLIP WILSON

What makes the desert beautiful... is that somewhere it hides a well.

ANTOINE DE SAINT-EXUPÉRY

IF YOU LOOK THE
RIGHT WAY, YOU CAN
SEE THAT THE WHOLE
WORLD IS A GARDEN.

FRANCES HODGSON BURNETT

Life is like
photography;
we develop from
the negatives.

ANONYMOUS

You are never too old to
set another goal or to
dream a new dream.

LES BROWN

THERE IS NOTHING IMPOSSIBLE TO HIM WHO WILL TRY.

ALEXANDER THE GREAT

Expect problems
and eat them
for breakfast.

ALFRED A. MONTAPERT

Those who wish to sing
always find a song.

SWEDISH PROVERB

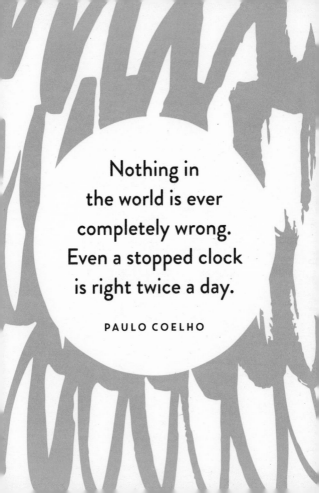

Nothing in
the world is ever
completely wrong.
Even a stopped clock
is right twice a day.

PAULO COELHO

I DON'T THINK OF ALL
THE MISERY, BUT OF
THE BEAUTY THAT
STILL REMAINS.

ANNE FRANK

Failures are like
skinned knees:
painful but
superficial.

ROSS PEROT

IN THE MIDDLE

OF DIFFICULTY

LIES OPPORTUNITY.

ALBERT EINSTEIN

Don't go through life,
grow through life.

ERIC BUTTERWORTH

MIGHTY OAKS
FROM LITTLE
ACORNS GROW.

ANONYMOUS

Laugh and the
world laughs
with you.

ELLA WHEELER WILCOX

Wherever you go, no matter what the weather, always bring your own sunshine.

ANTHONY J. D'ANGELO

ONE JOY SCATTERS

A HUNDRED GRIEFS.

CHINESE PROVERB

Enthusiasm
moves the world.

ARTHUR BALFOUR

IF YOU CAN'T GET
RID OF THE SKELETON
IN YOUR CLOSET,
YOU'D BEST TEACH
IT TO DANCE.

GEORGE BERNARD SHAW

Nothing is a
waste of time
if you use the
experience wisely.

AUGUSTE RODIN

To be without some of
the things you want
is an indispensable
part of happiness.

BERTRAND RUSSELL

It does not matter
how slowly you
go as long as you
do not stop.

CONFUCIUS

LOOK AT EVERYTHING
AS THOUGH YOU WERE
SEEING IT FOR THE
FIRST OR LAST TIME.

BETTY SMITH

When life looks like it's
falling apart, it may just
be falling in place.

BEVERLEY SOLOMON

IF YOU GIVE
PEOPLE A CHANCE,
THEY SHINE.

BILLY CONNOLLY

Every moment
has its pleasures
and its hope.

JANE AUSTEN

LIFE ISN'T ABOUT
WAITING FOR THE
STORM TO PASS; IT'S
ABOUT LEARNING TO
DANCE IN THE RAIN.

ANONYMOUS

THROW CAUTION TO THE WIND AND JUST DO IT.

CARRIE UNDERWOOD

Some people grumble
that roses have thorns;
I am grateful that
thorns have roses.

ALPHONSE KARR

THE MAN WHO
REMOVES A
MOUNTAIN BEGINS
BY CARRYING AWAY
SMALL STONES.

CHINESE PROVERB

All the statistics
in the world
can't measure the
warmth of a smile.

CHRIS HART

Happiness is not an ideal of reason, but of imagination.

IMMANUEL KANT

You live but once; you
might as well be amusing.

COCO CHANEL

IF YOU THINK YOU
ARE TOO SMALL TO
MAKE A DIFFERENCE,
TRY SLEEPING WITH
A MOSQUITO.

DALAI LAMA

There is always
room at the top.

DANIEL WEBSTER

The world is always open, waiting to be discovered.

DEJAN STOJANOVIĆ

Give light, and the darkness
will disappear of itself.

DESIDERIUS ERASMUS

WHEN ASKED IF MY
CUP IS HALF FULL
OR HALF EMPTY, MY
ONLY RESPONSE IS
THAT I AM THANKFUL
I HAVE A CUP.

ANONYMOUS

life shrinks
or expands in
proportion to
one's courage.

ANAÏS NIN

I may not have gone where I intended to go, but I think I have ended up where I needed to be.

DOUGLAS ADAMS

There are two ways of spreading light: to be the candle or the mirror that reflects it.

EDITH WHARTON

Ambition can creep
as well as soar.

EDMUND BURKE

BE GLAD OF LIFE
BECAUSE IT GIVES
YOU THE CHANCE TO
LOVE, TO WORK, TO
PLAY AND TO LOOK
UP AT THE STARS.

HENRY VAN DYKE

WITH THE NEW DAY

COMES NEW STRENGTH

AND NEW THOUGHTS.

ELEANOR ROOSEVELT

The sweetest pleasures
are those which are
hardest to be won.

GIACOMO CASANOVA

Perseverance is
failing nineteen
times and
succeeding
the twentieth.

JULIE ANDREWS

SOME DAYS THERE
WON'T BE A SONG
IN YOUR HEART.
SING ANYWAY.

EMORY AUSTIN

Plunge boldly into the thick of life, and seize it where you will, it is always interesting.

JOHANN WOLFGANG VON GOETHE

YOU CAN'T MAKE AN OMELETTE WITHOUT BREAKING EGGS.

ENGLISH PROVERB

Nothing is impossible, the word itself says 'I'm possible!'

AUDREY HEPBURN

START BY DOING
WHAT'S NECESSARY;
THEN DO WHAT'S
POSSIBLE; AND
SUDDENLY YOU
ARE DOING THE
IMPOSSIBLE.

FRANCIS OF ASSISI

Turn your face to the
sun and the shadows
fall behind you.

MAORI PROVERB

Positive anything is better
than negative nothing.

ELBERT HUBBARD

IT IS NEVER TOO LATE
TO BE WHAT YOU
MIGHT HAVE BEEN.

GEORGE ELIOT

If you can find
a path with
no obstacles, it
probably doesn't
lead anywhere.

FRANK A. CLARK

Find ecstasy in life;
the mere sense of
living is joy enough.

EMILY DICKINSON

No great thing is
created suddenly.

EPICTETUS

AERODYNAMICALLY
THE BUMBLEBEE
SHOULDN'T BE ABLE
TO FLY, BUT THE
BUMBLEBEE DOESN'T
KNOW SO IT GOES
FLYING ANYWAY.

MARY KAY ASH

Why not just live
in the moment,
especially if it has
a good beat?

GOLDIE HAWN

OPPORTUNITY DANCES WITH THOSE WHO ARE ALREADY ON THE DANCE FLOOR.

H. JACKSON BROWN JR

The important thing... is not how many years in your life, but how much life in your years!

EDWARD STIEGLITZ

FALL SEVEN TIMES, STAND UP EIGHT.

JAPANESE PROVERB

A happy life consists
not in the absence,
but in the mastery
of hardships.

HELEN KELLER

If you ask me what I came into this life to do, I will tell you: I came to live out loud.

ÉMILE ZOLA

It's never too late
– never too late to
start over, never too
late to be happy.

JANE FONDA

Smooth seas do not
make skilful sailors.

AFRICAN PROVERB

I THINK, WHAT HAS
THIS DAY BROUGHT
ME, AND WHAT
HAVE I GIVEN IT?

HENRY MOORE

One doesn't discover
new lands without
consenting to lose
sight of the shore
for a very long time.

ANDRÉ GIDE

Bad times have a scientific value. These are occasions a good learner would not miss.

RALPH WALDO EMERSON

I don't measure a
man's success by
how high he climbs
but how high he
bounces when he
hits bottom.

GEORGE S. PATTON

EVERY LOT HAS
ENOUGH HAPPINESS
PROVIDED FOR IT.

FYODOR DOSTOYEVSKY

Since the house is on fire
let us warm ourselves.

ITALIAN PROVERB

The sun is
new each day.

HERACLITUS

Mistakes are the
portals of discovery.

JAMES JOYCE

WHOEVER IS HAPPY
WILL MAKE OTHERS
HAPPY TOO.

ANNE FRANK

IF THINGS ARE GOING UNTOWARDLY ONE MONTH, THEY ARE SURE TO MEND THE NEXT.

JANE AUSTEN

He who has begun
is half done.

HORACE

WHEN YOU REACH
THE END OF YOUR
ROPE, TIE A KNOT IN
IT AND HANG ON.

THOMAS JEFFERSON

The roughest
road often leads
to the top.

CHRISTINA AGUILERA

I can't change the direction of the wind, but I can adjust my sails to always reach my destination.

JIMMY DEAN

IF WE HAD
NO WINTER,
THE SPRING
WOULD NOT BE
SO PLEASANT.

ANNE BRADSTREET

DARING IDEAS ARE
LIKE CHESSMEN
MOVED FORWARD.
THEY MAY BE BEATEN,
BUT THEY MAY START
A WINNING GAME.

JOHANN WOLFGANG VON GOETHE

Feelings are much like waves, we can't stop them from coming, but we can choose which ones to surf.

JONATAN MÅRTENSSON

Let your hook be always cast; in the pool where you least expect it, there will be fish.

OVID

May you live every
day of your life.

JONATHAN SWIFT

THE ROBBED THAT
SMILES, STEALS
SOMETHING FROM
THE THIEF.

WILLIAM SHAKESPEARE

Isn't it nice to think that tomorrow is a new day with no mistakes in it yet?

L. M. MONTGOMERY

Don't get your knickers in a knot. Nothing is solved and it just makes you walk funny.

KATHRYN CARPENTER

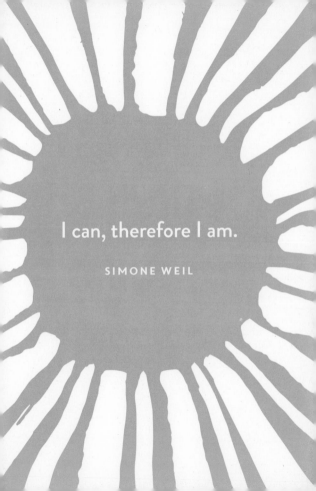

I can, therefore I am.

SIMONE WEIL

I'd rather regret
the things I've
done than regret
the things I
haven't done.

LUCILLE BALL

IF YOU LEARN FROM
DEFEAT, YOU HAVEN'T
REALLY LOST.

ZIG ZIGLAR

FOR EVERY MINUTE
YOU ARE ANGRY YOU
LOSE SIXTY SECONDS
OF HAPPINESS.

RALPH WALDO EMERSON

Never look backwards or you'll fall down the stairs.

RUDYARD KIPLING

If opportunity
doesn't knock,
build a door.

MILTON BERLE

THERE ARE ALWAYS
FLOWERS FOR
THOSE WHO WANT
TO SEE THEM.

HENRI MATISSE

Those who bring
sunshine into the lives
of others cannot keep
it from themselves.

J. M. BARRIE

Happiness often sneaks in through a door you didn't know you left open.

JOHN BARRYMORE

Opportunity often
comes disguised
in the form of
misfortune, or
temporary defeat.

NAPOLEON HILL

YOU CAN'T TURN
BACK THE CLOCK
BUT YOU CAN WIND
IT UP AGAIN.

BONNIE PRUDDEN

We are all in the gutter, but some of us are looking at the stars.

OSCAR WILDE

All great achievements
require time.

MAYA ANGELOU

OPPORTUNITIES MULTIPLY AS THEY ARE SEIZED.

SUN TZU

You can cut all the
flowers but you
cannot keep spring
from coming.

PABLO NERUDA

Our best successes often come after our greatest disappointments.

HENRY WARD BEECHER

Some days
you're the bug.
Some days you're
the windshield.

PRICE COBB

The sweetest pleasure arises
from difficulties overcome.

PUBLILIUS SYRUS

It is often in
the darkest skies
that we see the
brightest stars.

RICHARD EVANS

IF YOU'RE ALREADY

WALKING ON THIN ICE,

YOU MIGHT AS

WELL DANCE.

PROVERB

What we see depends
mainly on what we look for.

JOHN LUBBOCK

OPPORTUNITIES
DON'T OFTEN COME
ALONG. SO, WHEN
THEY DO, YOU HAVE
TO GRAB THEM.

AUDREY HEPBURN

Don't judge
each day by the
harvest you reap
but by the seeds
that you plant.

ROBERT LOUIS STEVENSON

There are no traffic jams
along the extra mile.

ROGER STAUBACH

VICTORY BELONGS
TO THE MOST
PERSEVERING.

NAPOLEON BONAPARTE

Do not think of
today's failures, but
of the success that
may come tomorrow.

HELEN KELLER

WHERE THERE IS
RUIN, THERE IS HOPE
FOR A TREASURE.

RUMI

The average pencil is seven inches long, with just a half-inch eraser — in case you thought optimism was dead.

ROBERT BRAULT

Life is a shipwreck, but we must not forget to sing in the lifeboats.

VOLTAIRE

Life isn't about
finding yourself.
Life is about
creating yourself.

GEORGE BERNARD SHAW

EVEN BEES, THE LITTLE
ALMSMEN OF SPRING
BOWERS, KNOW THERE
IS RICHEST JUICE IN
POISON-FLOWERS.

JOHN KEATS

WHO SEEKS

SHALL FIND.

SOPHOCLES

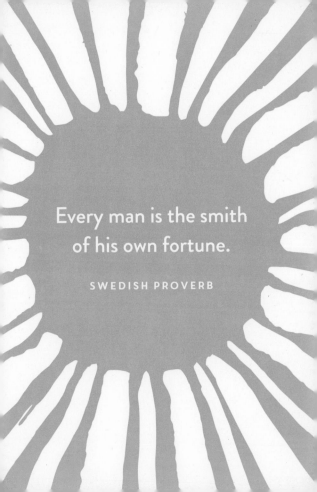

Every man is the smith
of his own fortune.

SWEDISH PROVERB

Only those who will risk going too far can possibly find out how far one can go.

T. S. ELIOT

REGARD MISTAKES AS TEACHERS, NOT JUDGES.

TAE YUN KIM

DO SOMETHING WONDERFUL. PEOPLE MAY IMITATE IT.

ALBERT SCHWEITZER

No life is so hard
that you can't make
it easier by the
way you take it.

ELLEN GLASGOW

VERY LITTLE IS
NEEDED TO MAKE
A HAPPY LIFE;
IT IS ALL WITHIN
YOURSELF, IN YOUR
WAY OF THINKING.

MARCUS AURELIUS

If we all did the things we are capable of, we would astound ourselves.

THOMAS EDISON

ALWAYS LAUGH
WHEN YOU CAN. IT IS
CHEAP MEDICINE.

LORD BYRON

The limits of the possible
can only be defined
by going beyond them
into the impossible.

ARTHUR C. CLARKE

A SMILE IS A FACELIFT
THAT'S IN EVERYONE'S
PRICE RANGE.

TOM WILSON

Everything is OK
in the end. If it's
not OK, then it's
not the end.

ANONYMOUS

Laugh as if it's funny, embrace as if it's love, and smile anyway.

RICHELLE E. GOODRICH

A gentle word, a kind look, a good-natured smile can work wonders and accomplish miracles.

WILLIAM HAZLITT

ANGELS CAN FLY
BECAUSE THEY TAKE
THEMSELVES LIGHTLY.

G. K. CHESTERTON

Act as if what
you do makes a
difference. It does.

WILLIAM JAMES

HOW WONDERFUL
IT IS THAT NOBODY
NEED WAIT A SINGLE
MOMENT BEFORE
STARTING TO
IMPROVE THE WORLD.

ANNE FRANK

For myself I am an optimist... it does not seem to be much use being anything else.

WINSTON CHURCHILL

A tree doesn't fall
with one blow.

YIDDISH PROVERB

IF YOU LOVE LIFE,
LIFE WILL LOVE
YOU BACK.

ARTHUR RUBINSTEIN

OUR GREATEST GLORY IS
NOT IN NEVER FALLING,
BUT IN RISING EVERY
TIME WE FALL.

CONFUCIUS

It just wouldn't be
a picnic without
the ants.

ANONYMOUS

Shoot for the
moon. Even if you
miss, you'll land
among the stars.

LES BROWN

NO ONE IS USELESS
IN THIS WORLD
WHO LIGHTENS
THE BURDENS
OF ANOTHER.

CHARLES DICKENS

The best is yet to do.

WILLIAM SHAKESPEARE

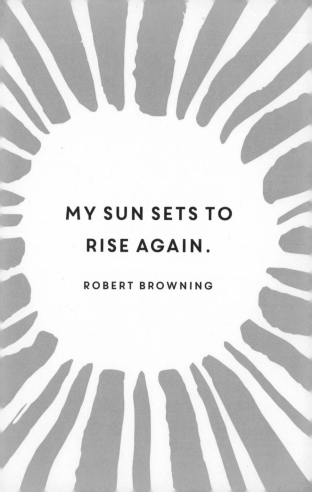

MY SUN SETS TO
RISE AGAIN.

ROBERT BROWNING

If you're interested in finding out more about our books, find us on Facebook at **Summersdale Publishers** and follow us on Twitter at @Summersdale.

www.summersdale.com